FAVORITE WEDDING SONGS

— PIANO LEVEL —
LATE INTERMEDIATE/EARLY ADVANCED

ISBN 978-1-4234-7795-2

HAL•LEONARD®
CORPORATION

7777 W. BLUEMOUND RD. P.O. BOX 13819 MILWAUKEE, WI 53213

Visit Hal Leonard Online at
www.halleonard.com

Visit Phillip at
www.phillipkeveren.com

PREFACE

This collection of wedding songs features 15 favorites that have become (or are becoming) standards over the last few decades. The beloved "Wedding Song (There Is Love)" is frequently heard at marriage ceremonies. "Highland Cathedral" is an elegant, stately piece that is not as well known, but is surely destined to be a classic. My personal favorite is "Gabriel's Oboe," a graceful melody that makes a perfect processional.

My hope is that this book offers you engaging choices as you select the music that will make your ceremony special.

Sincerely,
Phillip Keveren

BIOGRAPHY

Phillip Keveren, a multi-talented keyboard artist and composer, has composed original works in a variety of genres from piano solo to symphonic orchestra. Mr. Keveren gives frequent concerts and workshops for teachers and their students in the United States, Canada, Europe, and Asia. Mr. Keveren holds a B.M. in composition from California State University Northridge and a M.M. in composition from the University of Southern California.

CONTENTS

4 ALL I ASK OF YOU

8 DON'T KNOW MUCH

11 ENDLESS LOVE

14 GABRIEL'S OBOE

16 GROW OLD WITH ME

19 HALLELUJAH (YOUR LOVE IS AMAZING)

22 HIGHLAND CATHEDRAL

24 IN MY LIFE

28 LET IT BE ME (JE T'APPARTIENS)

31 MORE THAN WORDS

34 SEASONS OF LOVE

38 SUNRISE, SUNSET

41 THIS IS THE DAY (A WEDDING SONG)

48 WEDDING SONG (THERE IS LOVE)

44 YOU AND I

ALL I ASK OF YOU
from THE PHANTOM OF THE OPERA

Music by ANDREW LLOYD WEBBER
Lyrics by CHARLES HART
Additional Lyrics by RICHARD STILGOE
Arranged by Phillip Keveren

Flowing, deeply expressive (♩ = 76)

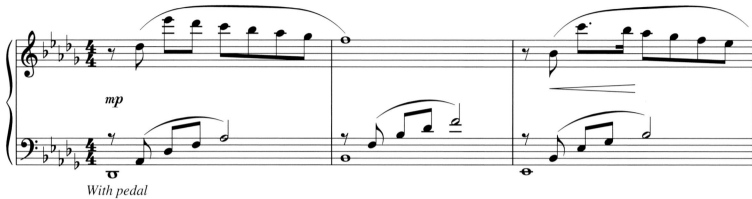

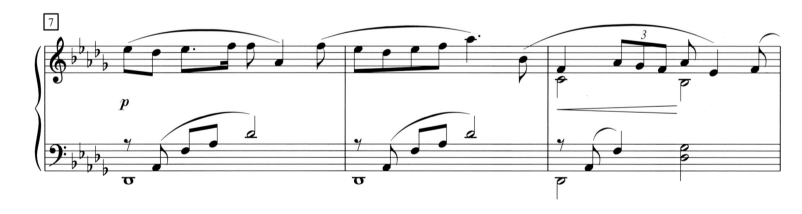

DON'T KNOW MUCH

Words and Music by BARRY MANN,
CYNTHIA WEIL and TOM SNOW
Arranged by Phillip Keveren

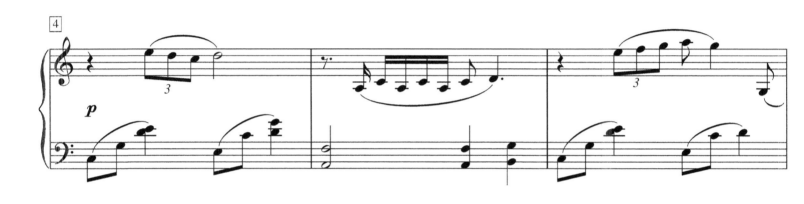

ENDLESS LOVE

from ENDLESS LOVE

Words and Music by
LIONEL RICHIE
Arranged by Phillip Keveren

GABRIEL'S OBOE
from the Motion Picture THE MISSION

Words and Music by
ENNIO MORRICONE
Arranged by Phillip Keveren

Slowly (♩ = 48-54)

p

expressively, with freedom

With pedal

cresc.

mf

dim. e rit.

GROW OLD WITH ME

Words and Music by
JOHN LENNON
Arranged by Phillip Keveren

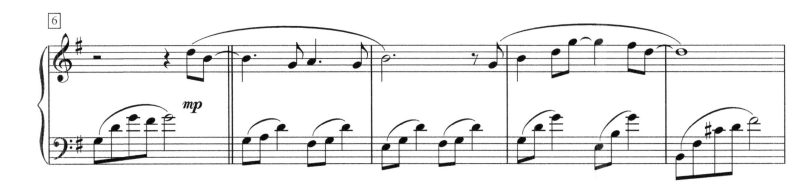

18

HALLELUJAH
(Your Love Is Amazing)

Words and Music by BRENTON BROWN
and BRIAN DOERKSEN
Arranged by Phillip Keveren

HIGHLAND CATHEDRAL

By MICHAEL KORB
and ULRICH ROEVER
Arranged by Phillip Keveren

Stately March ($\quad$ = 48)

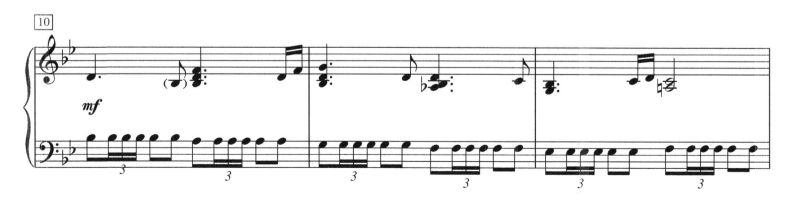

IN MY LIFE

Words and Music by JOHN LENNON
and PAUL McCARTNEY
Arranged by Phillip Keveren

Allegretto (♩ = 108)

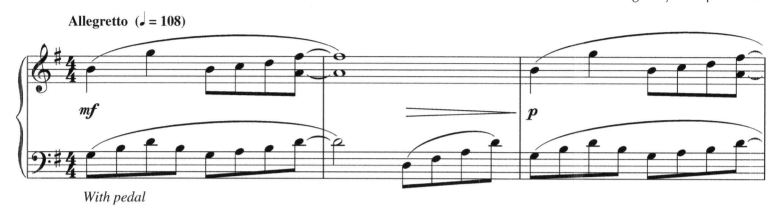

With pedal

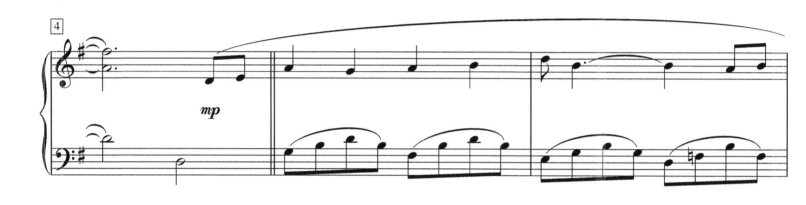

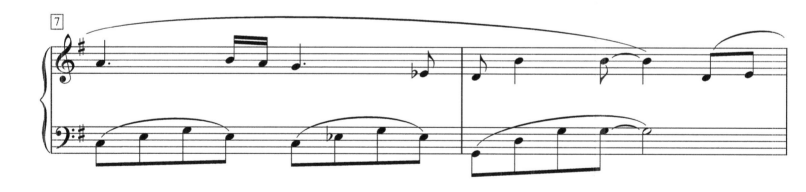

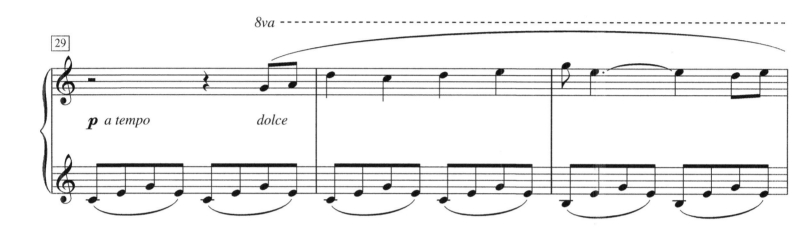

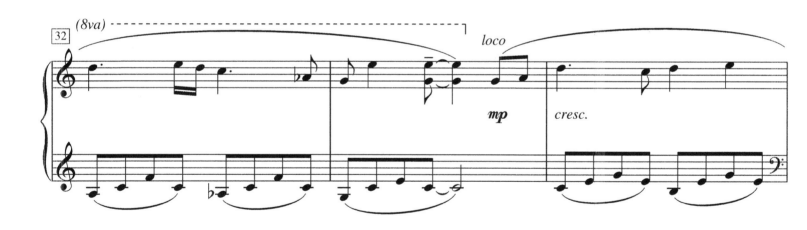

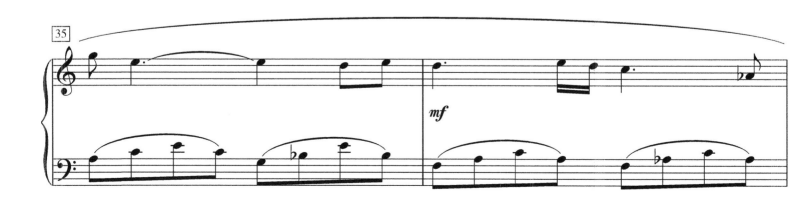

LET IT BE ME
(Je T'appartiens)

English Words by MANN CURTIS
French Words by PIERRE DeLANOE
Music by GILBERT BECAUD
Arranged by Phillip Keveren

Gently flowing (♩ = 104)

With pedal

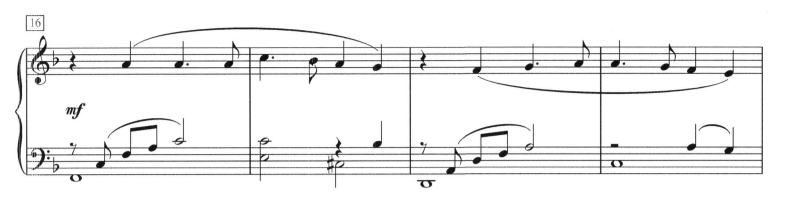

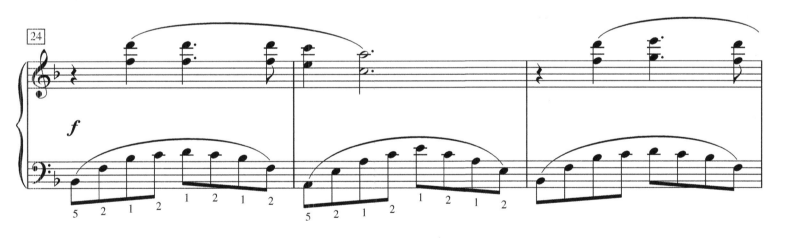

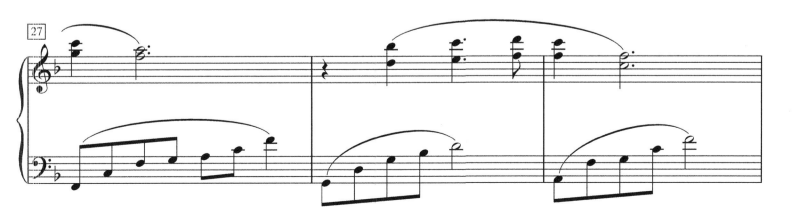

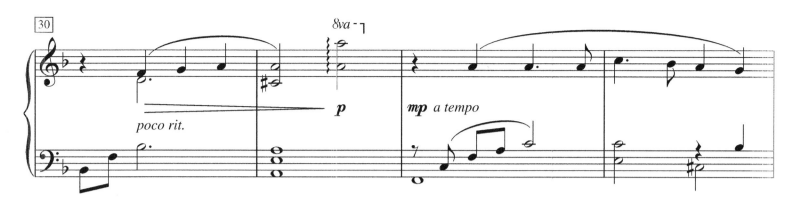

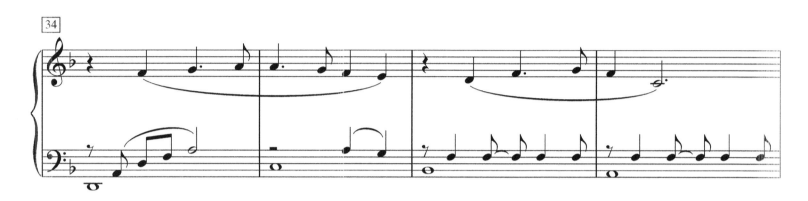

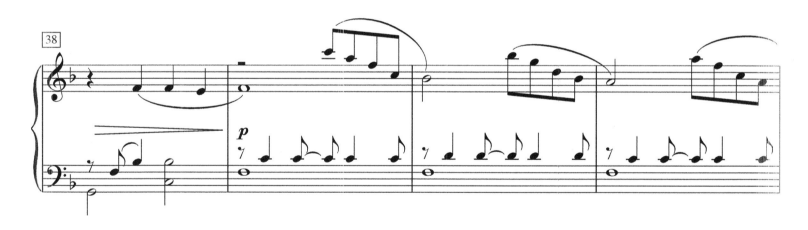

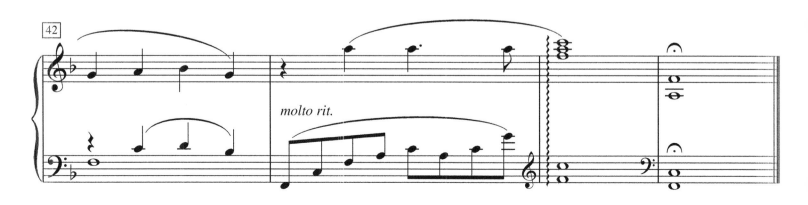

MORE THAN WORDS

Words and Music by NUNO BETTENCOURT
and GARY CHERONE
Arranged by Phillip Keveren

Tenderly (♩ = 108)

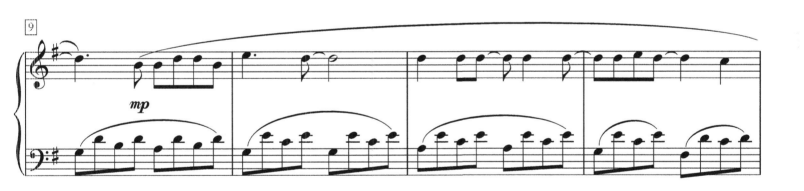

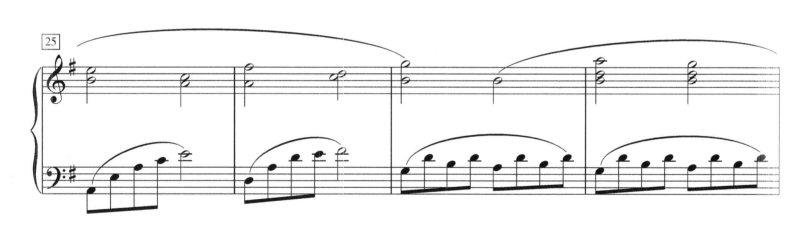

SEASONS OF LOVE
from RENT

Words and Music by
JONATHAN LARSON
Arranged by Phillip Keveren

SUNRISE, SUNSET
from the Musical FIDDLER ON THE ROOF

Words by SHELDON HARNICK
Music by JERRY BOCK
Arranged by Phillip Keveren

THIS IS THE DAY
(A Wedding Song)

Words and Music by
SCOTT WESLEY BROWN
Arranged by Phillip Keveren

YOU AND I

Words and Music by
FRANK MYERS
Arranged by Phillip Keveren

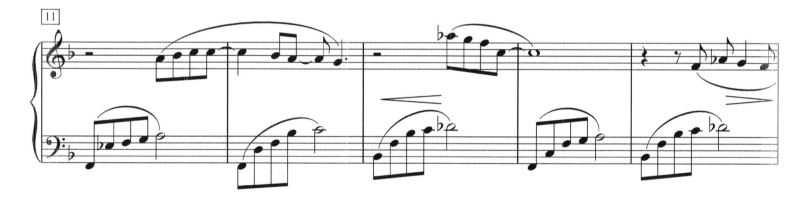

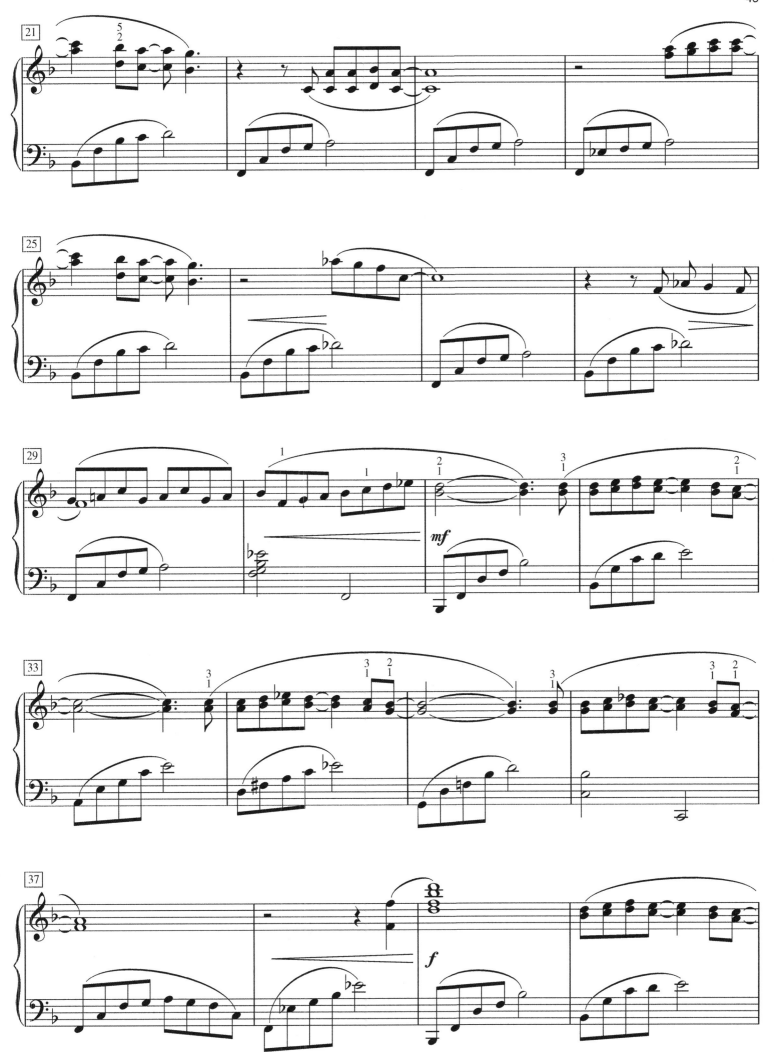

WEDDING SONG
(There Is Love)

Words and Music by
PAUL STOOKEY
Arranged by Phillip Keveren

Flowing (♩ = 108)

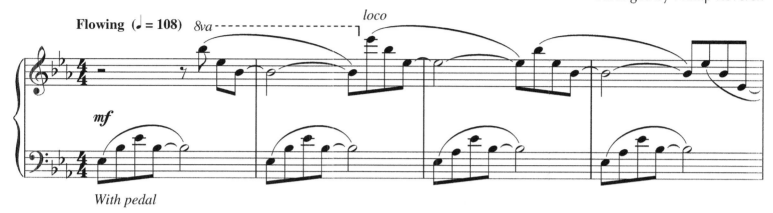

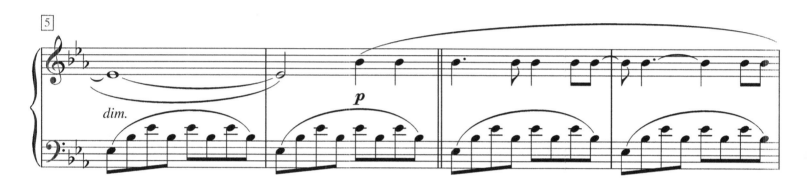

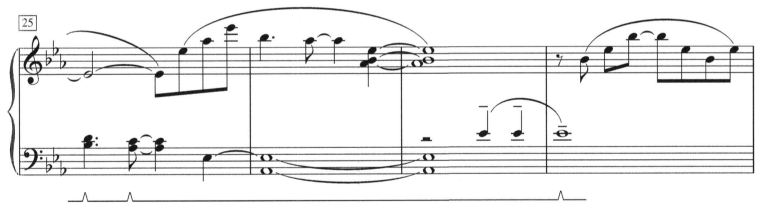

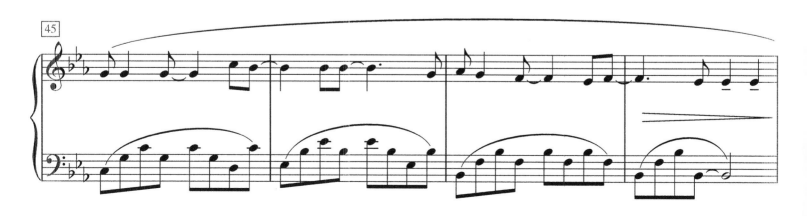

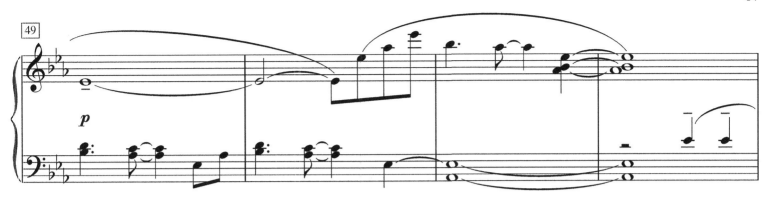

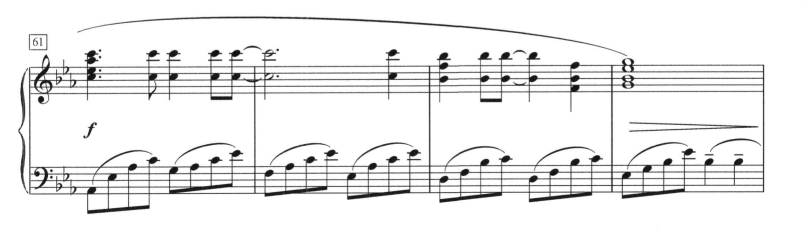

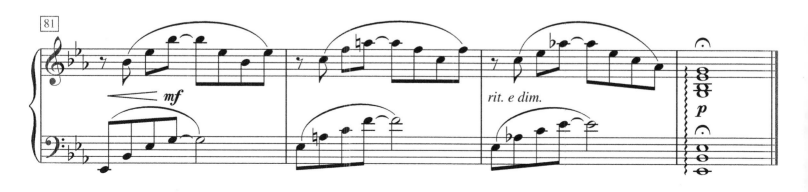

THE PHILLIP KEVEREN SERIES

HAL•LEONARD®

Search songlists, more products and place your order from your favorite music retailer at **halleonard.com**

PIANO SOLO

00156644	**ABBA for Classical Piano**	$15.99
00311024	**Above All**	$12.99
00311348	**Americana**	$12.99
00198473	**Bach Meets Jazz**	$14.99
00313594	**Bacharach and David**	$15.99
00306412	**The Beatles**	$19.99
00312189	**The Beatles for Classical Piano**	$17.99
00275876	**The Beatles – Recital Suites**	$19.99
00312546	**Best Piano Solos**	$15.99
00156601	**Blessings**	$14.99
00198656	**Blues Classics**	$14.99
00284359	**Broadway Songs with a Classical Flair**	$14.99
00310669	**Broadway's Best**	$16.99
00312106	**Canzone Italiana**	$12.99
00280848	**Carpenters**	$17.99
00310629	**A Celtic Christmas**	$14.99
00310549	**The Celtic Collection**	$14.99
00280571	**Celtic Songs with a Classical Flair**	$12.99
00263362	**Charlie Brown Favorites**	$14.99
00312190	**Christmas at the Movies**	$15.99
00294754	**Christmas Carols with a Classical Flair**	$12.99
00311414	**Christmas Medleys**	$14.99
00236669	**Christmas Praise Hymns**	$12.99
00233788	**Christmas Songs for Classical Piano**	$14.99
00311769	**Christmas Worship Medleys**	$14.99
00310607	**Cinema Classics**	$15.99
00301857	**Circles**	$10.99
00311101	**Classic Wedding Songs**	$12.99
00311292	**Classical Folk**	$10.95
00311083	**Classical Jazz**	$14.99
00137779	**Coldplay for Classical Piano**	$16.99
00311103	**Contemporary Wedding Songs**	$12.99
00348788	**Country Songs with a Classical Flair**	$14.99
00249097	**Disney Recital Suites**	$17.99
00311754	**Disney Songs for Classical Piano**	$17.99
00241379	**Disney Songs for Ragtime Piano**	$17.99
00364812	**The Essential Hymn Anthology**	$34.99
00311881	**Favorite Wedding Songs**	$14.99
00315974	**Fiddlin' at the Piano**	$12.99
00311811	**The Film Score Collection**	$15.99
00269408	**Folksongs with a Classical Flair**	$12.99
00144353	**The Gershwin Collection**	$14.99
00233789	**Golden Scores**	$14.99
00144351	**Gospel Greats**	$14.99
00183566	**The Great American Songbook**	$14.99
00312084	**The Great Melodies**	$14.99
00311157	**Great Standards**	$14.99
00171621	**A Grown-Up Christmas List**	$14.99
00311071	**The Hymn Collection**	$14.99
00311349	**Hymn Medleys**	$14.99
00280705	**Hymns in a Celtic Style**	$14.99
00269407	**Hymns with a Classical Flair**	$14.99
00311249	**Hymns with a Touch of Jazz**	$14.99
00310905	**I Could Sing of Your Love Forever**	$16.99
00310762	**Jingle Jazz**	$15.99
00175310	**Billy Joel for Classical Piano**	$16.99
00126449	**Elton John for Classical Piano**	$19.99
00310839	**Let Freedom Ring!**	$12.99
00238988	**Andrew Lloyd Webber Piano Songbook**	$14.99
00313227	**Andrew Lloyd Webber Solos**	$17.99
00313523	**Mancini Magic**	$16.99
00312113	**More Disney Songs for Classical Piano**	$16.99
00311295	**Motown Hits**	$14.99
00300640	**Piano Calm**	$12.99
00339131	**Piano Calm: Christmas**	$14.99
00346009	**Piano Calm: Prayer**	$14.99
00306870	**Piazzolla Tangos**	$17.99
00386709	**Praise and Worship for Classical Piano**	$14.99
00156645	**Queen for Classical Piano**	$17.99
00310755	**Richard Rodgers Classics**	$17.99
00289545	**Scottish Songs**	$12.99
00119403	**The Sound of Music**	$16.99
00311978	**The Spirituals Collection**	$12.99
00366023	**So Far...**	$14.99
00210445	**Star Wars**	$16.99
00224738	**Symphonic Hymns for Piano**	$14.99
00366022	**Three-Minute Encores**	$16.99
00279673	**Tin Pan Alley**	$12.99
00312112	**Treasured Hymns for Classical Piano**	$15.99
00144926	**The Twelve Keys of Christmas**	$14.99
00278486	**The Who for Classical Piano**	$16.99
00294036	**Worship with a Touch of Jazz**	$14.99
00311911	**Yuletide Jazz**	$19.99

EASY PIANO

00210401	**Adele for Easy Classical Piano**	$17.99
00310610	**African-American Spirituals**	$12.99
00218244	**The Beatles for Easy Classical Piano**	$14.99
00218387	**Catchy Songs for Piano**	$12.99
00310973	**Celtic Dreams**	$12.99
00233686	**Christmas Carols for Easy Classical Piano**	$14.99
00311126	**Christmas Pops**	$16.99
00368199	**Christmas Reflections**	$14.99
00311548	**Classic Pop/Rock Hits**	$14.99
00310769	**A Classical Christmas**	$14.99
00310975	**Classical Movie Themes**	$12.99
00144352	**Disney Songs for Easy Classical Piano**	$14.99
00311093	**Early Rock 'n' Roll**	$14.99
00311997	**Easy Worship Medleys**	$14.99
00289547	**Duke Ellington**	$14.99
00160297	**Folksongs for Easy Classical Piano**	$12.99

00110374	**George Gershwin Classics**	$14.99
00310805	**Gospel Treasures**	$14.99
00306821	**Vince Guaraldi Collection**	$19.99
00160294	**Hymns for Easy Classical Piano**	$14.99
00310798	**Immortal Hymns**	$12.99
00311294	**Jazz Standards**	$12.99
00355474	**Living Hope**	$14.99
00310744	**Love Songs**	$14.99
00233740	**The Most Beautiful Songs for Easy Classical Piano**	$12.99
00220036	**Pop Ballads**	$14.99
00311406	**Pop Gems of the 1950s**	$12.95
00233739	**Pop Standards for Easy Classical Piano**	$12.99
00102887	**A Ragtime Christmas**	$12.99
00311293	**Ragtime Classics**	$14.99
00312028	**Santa Swings**	$14.99
00233688	**Songs from Childhood for Easy Classical Piano**	$12.99
00103258	**Songs of Inspiration**	$14.99
00310840	**Sweet Land of Liberty**	$12.99
00126450	**10,000 Reasons**	$16.99
00310712	**Timeless Praise**	$14.99
00311086	**TV Themes**	$14.99
00310717	**21 Great Classics**	$14.99
00160076	**Waltzes & Polkas for Easy Classical Piano**	$12.99
00145342	**Weekly Worship**	$17.99

BIG-NOTE PIANO

00310838	**Children's Favorite Movie Songs**	$14.99
00346000	**Christmas Movie Magic**	$12.99
00277368	**Classical Favorites**	$12.99
00277370	**Disney Favorites**	$14.99
00310888	**Joy to the World**	$12.99
00310908	**The Nutcracker**	$12.99
00277371	**Star Wars**	$16.99

BEGINNING PIANO SOLOS

00311202	**Awesome God**	$14.99
00310837	**Christian Children's Favorites**	$14.99
00311117	**Christmas Traditions**	$10.99
00311250	**Easy Hymns**	$12.99
00102710	**Everlasting God**	$10.99
00311403	**Jazzy Tunes**	$10.95
00310822	**Kids' Favorites**	$12.99
00367778	**A Magical Christmas**	$14.99
00338175	**Silly Songs for Kids**	$9.99

PIANO DUET

00126452	**The Christmas Variations**	$14.99
00362562	**Classic Piano Duets**	$14.99
00311350	**Classical Theme Duets**	$12.99
00295099	**Gospel Duets**	$12.99
00311544	**Hymn Duets**	$14.99
00311203	**Praise & Worship Duets**	$14.99
00294755	**Sacred Christmas Duets**	$14.99
00119405	**Star Wars**	$16.99
00253545	**Worship Songs for Two**	$12.99

Prices, contents, and availability subject to change without notice.

0422
158

YOUR FAVORITE MUSIC
ARRANGED FOR PIANO SOLO

    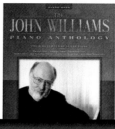 

ARTIST, COMPOSER, TV & MOVIE SONGBOOKS

Adele for Piano Solo
00307585.................................. $17.99

The Beatles Piano Solo
00294023.................................. $17.99

A Charlie Brown Christmas
00313176.................................. $17.99

Paul Cardall – The Hymns Collection
00295925.................................. $24.99

Coldplay for Piano Solo
00307637.................................. $17.99

Selections from Final Fantasy
00148699.................................. $19.99

Alexis Ffrench – The Sheet Music Collection
00345258.................................. $19.99

Game of Thrones
00199166.................................. $19.99

Hamilton
00354612.................................. $19.99

Hillsong Worship Favorites
00303164.................................. $14.99

How to Train Your Dragon
00138210.................................. $22.99

Elton John Collection
00306040.................................. $24.99

La La Land
00283691.................................. $14.99

John Legend Collection
00233195.................................. $17.99

Les Misérables
00290271.................................. $19.99

Little Women
00338470.................................. $19.99

Outlander: The Series
00254460.................................. $19.99

The Peanuts® Illustrated Songbook
00313178.................................. $29.99

Astor Piazzolla – Piano Collection
00285510.................................. $19.99

Pirates of the Caribbean – Curse of the Black Pearl
00313256.................................. $19.99

Pride & Prejudice
00123854.................................. $17.99

Queen
00289784.................................. $19.99

John Williams Anthology
00194555.................................. $24.99

George Winston Piano Solos
00306822.................................. $22.99

    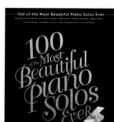 

MIXED COLLECTIONS

Beautiful Piano Instrumentals
00149926.................................. $16.99

Best Jazz Piano Solos Ever
00312079.................................. $24.99

Best Piano Solos Ever
00242928.................................. $19.99

Big Book of Classical Music
00310508.................................. $24.99

Big Book of Ragtime Piano
00311749.................................. $22.99

Christmas Medleys
00350572.................................. $16.99

Disney Medleys
00242588.................................. $17.99

Disney Piano Solos
00313128.................................. $17.99

Favorite Pop Piano Solos
00312523.................................. $16.99

Great Piano Solos
00311273.................................. $16.99

The Greatest Video Game Music
00201767.................................. $19.99

Most Relaxing Songs
00233879.................................. $17.99

Movie Themes Budget Book
00289137.................................. $14.99

100 of the Most Beautiful Piano Solos Ever
00102787.................................. $29.99

100 Movie Songs
00102804.................................. $29.99

Peaceful Piano Solos
00286009.................................. $17.99

Piano Solos for All Occasions
00310964.................................. $24.99

River Flows in You & Other Eloquent Songs
00123854.................................. $17.99

Sunday Solos for Piano
00311272.................................. $17.99

Top Hits for Piano Solo
00294635.................................. $14.99

HAL•LEONARD®
View songlists online and order from your favorite music retailer at
halleonard.com